Lucy Dougan | The Guardians

New Poems

GIRAMONDO POETS

Lucy Dougan | The Guardians

First Published 2015
from the Writing & Society Research Centre
at the University of Western Sydney
by the Giramondo Publishing Company
PO Box 752 Artarmon NSW 1570 Australia
www.giramondopublishing.com

Designed by Harry Williamson
Typeset by Andrew Davies
In 10/16pt Baskerville

Printed and bound by Ligare Book Printers
Distributed in Australia by NewSouth Books

National Library of Australia
Cataloguing-in-Publication data:

Dougan, Lucy
The Guardians / Lucy Dougan
ISBN 978-1-922146-75-5 (pbk.)
A821.3

For Julia

Other books by Lucy Dougan

Memory Shell
The Forest Waits (with Andrew Taylor & Kevin Gillam)
White Clay
On the Circumvesuviana
Meanderthals
Against Lawns

Acknowledgements

I am grateful to the editors of the following anthologies and journals in which many of the poems first appeared: *Australian Book Review, Australian Literary Review, Australian Love Poems, Blast, Best Australian Poems 2008, 2009, 2010, 2014, Cordite, Famous Reporter, Five Bells, Island, Medical Journal of Australia, Perihelion Review, Southerly, Warwick Review, Westerly, Women's Work, the wonderbook*. Some of the poems have been published in the chapbooks *The Forest Waits, On the Circumvesuviana, Meanderthals, Against Lawns*.

Warm thanks for their encouragement to: Carolyn Abbs, Gerri Cox, Tim Dolin, Jenny Dougan, Lesley Dougan, Susan Fealy, Aaron Hales, Kerry Hardie, Paul Hetherington, Rozanna Lilley, Ivor Indyk, Jean Kent, Sally Scott and Fay Zwicky. Special thanks for desk space provided by Neil Levi and Beth Drenning, and the Faculty of Arts & Design, University of Canberra. And to Tim, Jules and Aaron for summer weeks in the cottage at Lower Bockhampton.

Contents

1

2

3

1

There are sounds and there are spaces.
Human creatures could have left long ago
ELIZABETH JENNINGS, 'Celebration of Winter'

The Mask

This is the house of her childhood.
It's not standing anymore.
And in that house she slept
in a long thin room
in the bed for the youngest
against a bank of dimpled louvres
that broke up all the leaf shapes outside
so that they patterned
the patch of floor on which she played.

Below the place she slept
was a room beneath the house
and from that room
one summer
her mother had dragged out an old brown trunk.
Perhaps it held the other life of the house, she had said,
but to her child's eye its contents gave disappointment.

There were tatty papers
curling at the edges,
things that someone had begun to knit
and given up on.
Beneath this tangle something lay
that her mother snatched up quickly.
It was a face made of linen.
There were eye-holes, and a mouth
and they took turns in it

running crazily about the garden.
But she already hated it,
had relinquished it to the grass
where it lay, she imagined, sulking.

Breathless, she asked who made it.

Probably my nanna, said her mother.

Oh, was all she managed to say back.

That night she wondered
if there were more rooms
beneath the room under her bed.
How deep did they go down;
and if each of her mother's mothers
stretching right back
had left a fearful face there
for her to try on?

Poem on All Souls' Day

You put your arms out of the covers
in the cold night air
just to say you are not scared,
to say fuck off to the horror.
The wind carries the sound of a train
or is that some old other
rat-a-tat? – foolish to think
that your stubborn body
with its genetic hand-me-downs
is not implicated,
is not the haunted house.
And how we just have to go
and do it all again;
how, one way or another,
we have all always been here.
Even now your pulse starts and stops
in the maze of your veins,
its wrong turns to dead-ends
branching this way and that,
someone's feet and not your own
doubling back in the snow.

Atavism I

Squatting in the kitchen
I share leftover lamb with the cat.
It is as if he were a bad fellow
returned from some wrongdoing.
I think for a moment that he will confess
and I will absolve him
with these bits from the body
of another animal.

Our meat communion is slight and stringy,
it coats our tongues with fat.
He mews. I mutter. It's over,
this blurring of boundaries
between fur and skin.
But I feel in the house somewhere
a lean cat man with a grudge,
slipping off his boots,
bent on retribution.

Atavism II

Somerset St Swimming Pool

That boy lazing
in the truth
of his tattoos
(deep inside himself
deep inside the way light
from the sheet of water
talks to the ceiling)
and in the change-room
small shoes
side by side
with the larger pair
that walked here
with them.

Bodies tiled in place:
a man mid-dive,
a woman alert to a child,
each attitude repeating
an anonymous civic grace
old as the mosaics
we have uncovered.

At Villa Bruno

At Villa Bruno
the presiding nymph
has black texta circles
around all her bits.
She watches us
with her nipples, her navel,
as we trail on opposite sides
of the long garden bed,
swapping names:
my bay for your *lauro*,
your *arancia* for my orange,
until our paths meet.
We fall into the spaciousness
of another century.
We might have trailing skirts, masks.
I take the crushed leaves, the proffered fruit,
and feel the blind nymph's
cool bemusement
as we step outside all drawn rings.
Nothing before
has tasted so close
to its wild estate.

The Mice

my mother took them to the river
with a packet of weet-bix
their carousel – that scampering
roundabout of *Who am I?* –
their dense burrow smell
I could add them to the list
of things with which I never played
gifts from my wayward father
that were out-of-bounds
the idea of mouse – a rumour
frantic in abandoned parts –
she unlatched the cage and said
kids, you're on your own

but they come back
these feral colonies
I could not tend
they come back
with their cold little paws
we've been away for such a long time they chant
they are the chorus of what could have been

when I was a child
story books were full of mice
their thin limbs poking from dimity smocks
and neat waistcoats
lost mice – untraceable country cousins

that stretch of land by the river
it really was wild
a wasteland then
we lay in clumps of bamboo
and smoked our first cigarettes
bamboo bumsuckers
the lost mice clamoured inside
my headspins
the priests came down
to practice their golf
they gave us their soft Irish voices
glimpses of secular ankles
as they pulled up their cassocks
to wade into swampy land
we retrieved their lost golf balls
and with the rewards
bought more cigarettes
holy cigarettes
taboos were built into everything
that happened in the clumps

the other day
I went back for the mice
and saw a man sitting
on a fold-out chair
just at the edge
of where it used to be wild
he faced away from the view
towards the road

I wanted to pull over
and not exactly talk to him
just reclaim a little rank whiff
from the poshed-up frontage
there was something wrong
with the man
he seemed to be doing an imitation
of a man sitting in the sun
like me
the place was lost on him.

Wayside

I know that it is by being unknown to myself, that I live
HÉLÈNE CIXOUS

My body wants
the long way back
just to find lost land
rehearsing what it will be –
unexpected flowerings
locked tight in seeds.

I have searched for this
as one seeks origin:
to find the errant sower
jaunty in a book of days,
the uncertain map
of family trees.

It is that ur-place
of first collections –
black furred caterpillars,
glass jars and grass rash,
time in suspension,
place as mood.

Seeds in my pocket
put me in mind
of the strange, small plants
we grew in the cupboard –

an experiment
that claimed my pity.

And of my *nipote*,
a love child too,
who took me aside
and mimed at fireworks
with hands and eyes,
his fingers sprays.

We're like this, you see,
all kaboom and splutter –
who knows where we'll fall.
Somewhere between
Piazza Dante and Piazza Gesù
is all I am told.

My body wants
the dark of a city
when paths were lit
by shrines, by love,
their frail flames
petals no-one owns.

1988

for my sister Jenny

Baby Face

I close my eyes to the pattern of ivy on a wall in
negative – the film of the day replayed – and when
I hear your voice you're saying Don't people look
like babies when they sleep, somehow the face falls
back to what it was before. Your hand trails my hair.
So surely have I grown after you – one foot, two –
I've followed you here to the furthest point from
home where all the road signs read haste ye back.
Somehow we've come further back, to the time you
watched over my cot. We've lain in hotels at night
and listened to the harried steps of women alone,
asked questions of the dark as much about ourselves
as the footsteps we don't own. South from here
in London you slept with a picture of the young
Mendelssohn above your bed because it kept my face
clear in your dreams. It was stuck next to the legend:
Gee Toto, I don't think we're in Kansas anymore.

Heights

At St Paul's we played at sisters, played at symmetry
and duplications, played at the little princes in
velvet doublets. As one figure runs towards a mirror,
we took separate entrances and sent our pledges
shinnying around the curves of the whispering
wall. Your secrets were all lapping wings and I
met you breathless in the centre, transfixed by the
checkerboard bulls-eye below. I held you back from
an imagined fall, sensed it because I am like that too.
When one asked did you ever and the other said
never – that was a lie –

Old Sarum

At the walls of Old Sarum we meet ourselves.
Down below are our two silver heads bent together.
Naturally we are curious on the eve of our
humanness, the five children to come. We tucked a
note in the ruins to remind ourselves that on this day
in forty years we will return – our wallets lined with
the concertinaed faces of grandchildren we cannot
imagine – our skins as paper.

The Shy Dog

Our customary visible order is not the only one. It coexists with other orders...Hunters are continually aware of it...Dogs, with their running legs, sharp noses and developed memory for sounds, are the natural experts of these interstices. JOHN BERGER

The shy dog will only come to me,
to a female voice.
The vet says it's all down to the kennels,
her handler.
My fingers explore the small ridges of her skull
and we are shifting into a landscape of grasses,
moving with the tribe.
Or, I am very young again
and up in the attic
reading Henry Treece;
travelling for days with the men,
never leaving my bed.
The Icini queen burns London, Colchester, Verlamion
and claims the hero with swinging plait and blue skin,
her palm warm on his thigh.
Later, I tried this move on a boyfriend
but he didn't, like the hound, take me for a natural leader.
At least this...
My son, who is currently berserker,
would have some place out beyond the dog,
a forward scout,
crazy enough to take the necessary risks.
And I think, too, of my father's death.

How removed we are from that fierce place
except for the *Discovery Channel*.
I wanted a bier, fire.
I wanted to decorate with gold teeth, spoils
he told me to claim at the end.
With the shy dog,
watchful for my next command,
maybe I could just have done that.

Sewing the Dog

This was the stitching that Ned helped her finish.
It was on holidays,
                    one of the last holidays
when the children still seemed children.
She had been moved by a boy's eagerness.
You see – it goes like this – take it through
on the diagonal and then to the next space behind –
yes – that's it – just like that.
Appearing before their eyes was the running hound
with the French words around the pedestrian border
that would not be filled in
(perversely she liked this bit best)
and all the little clumps of flowers
through which the creature ran.
Months from now her brother-in-law
will bury the dog
they had all loved;
the dog the twin of this one
in the tapestry they are finishing.
It was French
like all good painted canvasses for stitching.
She found it in the throw-out bin
at the door in the craft shop
that had been on the corner for years
in which the people were unfriendly.
He would bury the dog
in just this pose

with her feet thrust out running
and, although not given to sentiment,
he would say
as he closed the earth over
there – you will always be running
but now,
                now
the woman and the boy
pull the wool through
and she runs her hands through his hair suddenly
and says *you're good at this*
you could finish it
if you put your mind to it.

Submariners' Bell

The vitrine lit up
like the cinematic organs
of extra-terrestrials;
in this other, submariner world
the children's reflections cluster,
clumps of rare corals.
Their cheekbones, brows and chins
go to water.

Years since, their names are forgotten
but I remember the sturdy bell.
It, too, seemed submerged,
as full of portent as those stories
of drowned villages
with their tolling auditory hallucinations.
The bell's contours warped our likenesses.

On its inner rim were engraved
all the names of the mariners' children born to land
when their fathers worked beneath the waves.
It was a prerogative to choose them
and ring them out
beyond the ken
of the ones who would carry them
down the years.

Our group moved on.
The silent bell kept its record
and our faces wavered briefly
on museum glass, were drowned
and replaced.

The Forge

The women in these suburbs
flirt with the man who cuts keys, fixes heels.
They can't help being won over
by the light that glowers at his shop-front.
Too sure of himself by half
my mother would say.
He dyes his hair unflatteringly dark.
Once I took him shoes,
a second-hand pair.
God, love, he asked,
what have you been doing in these?
I laugh at the histories I could invent
for these strangers – sleep-walking, bacchic dance.
I laugh and say nothing
as he hands me the little green slip.
But I don't go back for a long, long time
(life more ruptured than the wreck
of shoes I handed him, impossible to unlock).
Where you been darl?
(if I could click my heels).
It's a story I cannot tell –
what kept me from redeeming
something fixed.
At night the women in these suburbs
unlock their doors
with keys fashioned
by the man at the kiosk.

They kick off their shoes
shiny and re-heeled.
They smile without quite knowing
how the man with the dark, dark hair
has eased his way into their smallest secret places,
snug in the palm, firm at the ankle.
And I chide myself gently
for not telling him the story of the book
I swapped for shoes
or why I had been away for so long.

Julia, Reading

Belly down on the graveyard lawn,
you balance the court shoe
you have just thrown off
neatly between two feet,
engrossed in a book
with your father's reading face on.
Small white flowers dot the lawn
and the gravestones, leaning
willy-nilly like bad old teeth,
stretch beyond you.
Here the parish let the place go wild,
left hides for foxes,
free passage for any number
of skittering things.
Good, we think, these dead are not lonely.
And I love it that you can
lie here on the grass so casually alive
and lost, no doubt, in some current franchise.
The small of your back is just bare
and the soles of your feet catch the light.

Now your feet have outgrown
these kitten heels,
sensible purchase from a stalwart aunt,
so I wore them all next winter
in another hemisphere,
walked the thin lining of black suede

off their backs.
They are good for gardening,
dashes to the shops;
and I find I cannot throw them out
because in them rest
your hair glints on that day,
a big untidy bunch of yellow flowers
left by a grave,
and St Witta's bones at Canonicorum,
if you bound up suddenly,
just steps away.

A Patch

A picture of you all,
figures woven in a scene
of blackberry picking.
There's an impulse that passes through
arms, canes, turned shoulders, smiles,
and even the girls' hair
that flies free to catch in
bramble, thorn.
My father's mouth is crammed
not only with fruit
but the moment.
This is not a shot
with which to play the merciless game
and one will…and one will…and one will.
It needs to be freed
and given up eternally
to the one we can't see,
the one who caught it.
Now…and now…and now answers
one will – and also the time we stalked
the bottom of the Giant's feet
and found all the berries in another place.
One liked to pick and one to eat;
a perfect arrangement,
as when years back
my sister and I had sat
on the self-same Giant

and asked for children.
Here they are then manifest:
trailing, picking, eating
– wondrously alive –
and here they are before
in a sideways patch,
their grandparents and great aunt,
mouths crammed,
genetics sparking magnetically
along the lines.

2

Anywhere abandoned serves as a magnet
GEOFF DYER, *Zona*

London, Misbooked

Up and up the stairs, dragging my load
to a narrow arrangement beneath leaded windows.
First, case in front of the bed
and then a kind of leap is what it took,
all of it unreal as the miles just flown.
Another leap off the end to the closet bathroom and
I was getting to know the cramped proportions
of old lives in this little eyrie.
I lay sprawled on the bed
like the pale skinned fraudster poet
only I was no marvellous boy
but reasonably along in life
with a full head of strangely curled hair
(perhaps our only likeness) after the drugs.
And I didn't die
but watched tele, something with Shirley Henderson in it,
filled out the breakfast order,
let the unaccustomed night fall on me.
Near sleep I thought this is probably the maid's room
but I didn't have to get up and do for anyone in the morning.
The doves came down to see me
and cooed their own flight histories
into my jetlagged limbs,
and if they were forgeries, too,
a human ear could not tell.

Kenwood House

The lip-gloss tastes of heritage London,
its flavour something berry hedgerow
and the rainy day we took shelter
in the house on the heath.
Its walls were lined with Jacobeans –
nobody knows who these people were,
the guide says simply.
Long, knowing faces like Donne's
square up with the smudgy day outside.
I want to say tippets and lappets
and *words like paduasoy*, so marvellous
is the material world of these ghosts.
Their bodies seethe with witty details.
We taste cider, get lost in passages;
the carpet does a bad cover-up job
of all the feet it's taken.
I ask you if we bumped into Donne
or Shakespeare or their wives
(especially their wives
I would want to meet)
could we all make sense?
And you said, *of course,*
they are early moderns.
Back out on the heath
more fine rain,
more ghosts.

Coleridge warbling
behind his doctor's back
to the nervous apothecary's boy
in the alleyway,
anxious for another draught.

Tate Modern

Bourgeois' *Maman*
her spider mother
crouches diabolically over London
you can walk right in to the gallery
through the sinister entrance
of her legs
it's that game all children play
making the miniature monstrous
inside you can line up
and buy handkerchiefs
bearing the legend
I've been to hell
and back
and I can tell you
it was wonderful
all that satin stitch
would be hard on a nose
with a cold I thought
and then of coffee long ago
with an arts bureaucrat
sod the exhibition
let's cut to the merch
merch here, I discover,
is a kind of love talk
and I am requisitely seduced
by two pink magnets
art is a guarantee of sanity claims one,

the other commands *be calm*
then joke with the man in the line
behind me who wants to buy
be calm too
that we got spat out of the exhibition
at a video spool of the artist
dismantling her studio
in rock-god style
he holds the magnet up
to the glossy indifference
of the Thames
like I need this
he laughs
do you?

The Foxes

The first night back
– long Northern nights –
in the room on the upper-storey
at Westbourne Grove
with the dangerous slope.

We stood at the deep sash window
and beneath us
two foxes stared up.
Their gaze was not territorial
or neutral but simply there

as the grass was there, the trees
were there, and the old summer furniture.
They did not hide their boredom
and crossed back over
into another evening.

But we stayed for a while
as if their candour held us to the spot
until lights started up
– those other unknown lives –
in the flats across.

On C Leaving Suddenly

It could be traced to the census
that you lived here with the boy – for what?
a year – although it felt much longer.
My first glimpse of you –
a slender foot, beautifully and incongruously
poised on mossy bricks.
It was a scene from a book
that might have been called *Hymen Approaches*.
Then various sightings in the street:
I think that's her – and yes, that's her.
Your furtive visits to the mirror in the hall,
and your soundless retreats.
I learned your trust
as one might a wild injured thing's;
and when you left precipitously
I saw your face in a series of stills,
wan as a governess
who had travelled a perilous road,
all drenched skirts.
And I hope it is you
who has taken my dressing gown,
the summer one with lots of colours,
because at least some part of here
will still be holding you.

Nettle Soup

And then I think
I will just take off
because I am sick of your *merde*.
What gives me the idea?
You're running with a bad crowd,
who think the word juvie
has a cute ring to it
but at least they are stylish.
You bring home *Vogue Uomo*
and there's my escape
in a spread of pages:
nettle soup in big white bowls
with the sting cooked out.
I rewrite my life
in grass-green drizzle round the rim
as the hedgerows beckon.
The other ingredients
are not so hard on the hands.
A big skirt and a lupine-looking man,
an art directed caravan
with *Tom-Tom* on tap
so that when the soup gets thin
(and believe me, it will)
we can find our way
to the next stinging patch.

Kensal Green

We are searching for Wilkie Collins
when we see the fox
who is perfectly at home here;
his lively snow flecked tail, cardinal red,
brushes the lanes of the sentimental angels,
stands out like a guide's umbrella
against the huge black yews.
When you go down to the crypt
a man can't stop himself
from touching a casket's rotting velvet.
It comes away in his hands
you tell us. The guide castigates,
the man pockets it, shows no remorse
Above ground I stamp at the cold,
following Mr Fox
in hope that he will
show me what he knows
about the dead.
Slim pickings here
for him, and for us too.
I entice you back
to the land of the living,
Tea at Café Rouge?

Tower Bridge to Greenwich, 24.01.11

Nature herself who all created first,
Invented sowing, and the wild plants nurs't:
When mast and berries from the trees did drop,
Succeeded under by a numerous crop.
JOHN EVELYN, 'Sylva'

1

Tower Bridge to Greenwich,
the morning's blurry procession,
London's villages collapse behind us.
The Thames' banks are chalky at low tide,
a child's shoe, a lost glove – its hand-shape stiff with salt –
a piece of orange rope. Through Deptford
a tight, terrible feeling
moving near Marlowe's fate
until we fall, relieved and breathless,
into the untidy grid of Pepys Court.
A desolate decorum in this low-rise,
tufty, untended grass.
Yet here the ground falters, opens
into a cleared enclosure.
At its centre the oldest imaginable tree,
alive or dead is hard to say,
its roots, branches, and blackened bark
holding a pact with the elements
so the question is almost null.
We stand and take it in.
This important, fenced-off thing,

as one might linger in a zoo
and look and look at the last of its kind.
Later we know this as the antechamber
to a vast and disappeared garden.

2

We gain Greenwich steadily,
more lost stories on the way,
pulled through time
to its marshalling point
and arrive at a place
held up by sound.
At the opera master-class in Wren's church
the teacher is exacting.
Her charges' voices quake and right themselves,
notes half-reached, then earned.
We leave before the lesson ends.
Outside, a woman close to labour
swoons and rights herself
as the singers had just done.
She watches our children
chasing through the colonnades.
We joke that they're a lighter load
delivered to the world;
but then they are forever running.
We can never quite catch up.

3

We find we can afford the ferry home.
Aboard it's cold and we sit close.
Our walk dissolves, comes back
in the life inside the woman –
the flush of cheeks, the bright in her eyes.
She bestows the day's final O,
the dazzling way in which
the lights halo now on the river,
the dazzling way in which
genes that stretch right back
perpetuate, and how
the ruined tree
set darkly by the Thames,
that we will never find again,
still puts out its buds –
as the one who planted it
promised it would.

The Ties My Sister Makes

For Elena

The silk ties my sister makes
lie sheathed in plastic sheets
in their pigeonholes
in the factory
beneath the volcano.
They hold all the colours of the sea
and are scaled like fishes too
so that when I first see them
laid out in their obedient ranks
I want to exclaim like Willmouse
at the Roman fish market
Che belle cose.
My sister's ties
will be dispatched about the world,
their underwater silvers and greens
flashing in the dark aquariums of shop windows.
I think of all the necks they will encircle,
the men who will make their deft adjustments
and the women who will stroke them and roll them away
with socks or hang them inside wardrobe doors,
unaware of my sister's clever hands
and of her name
inside the label
beating out its syllables
silently next to their husband's hearts.

Guillemots

There's an intruder
in the cliff city
of the guillemots,
a seeker for eggs
of various speckled
greens and blues.
The stunt exists
to show us in our lounge-rooms
how much the Saxons
prized this protein.
You're just home.
I feel relieved
that you haven't
been scaling such heights,
even though you did
steal the indeterminate
colour of your eyes
from these lofty clutches.
You're just home
with the slightest reprimand
from your grandparents
for wearing the wrong clothes
suspended on the air,
a television sea-bird's call,
that diminishes now
as you turn those eyes to mine.
You do not stop looking at me.

I stroke your cheek
recalling a radio voice from the past:
They called it their tender time.
I reclaim you by this gaze,
your first gift to me,
and I know you by colour –
as a guillemot mother
exhausted from hunting
can return to her own eggs, hers alone,
in the hanging sea-bird citadel
on the high white cliffs.
There are no raiders yet
and you can wear
all the wrong clothes you want.
Beyond your cradled shoulder
I keep the intrepid egg thief
at a blurry distance.

Fritz

We would stop and he would ask the farmers if we could camp.
Then the children would be sent to collect wood.
We set small fires for the cooking
and a larger communal one
that the adults would retire to in the darkness,
whispering circular riddles to us
we could not replicate.
I had been assigned James
who was younger
with the bowl-cut of a prince.
When he did something particularly brave
or selfless, even in play,
I felt the first tinges of maternal satisfaction,
standing back with hands on hips,
shading my eyes
and saying, yes, that is good.
Yet I had not graduated.
I was somewhere in between
my charge and the fire,
fearing the jump.

Fritz sewed us into the earth in rows
and we lay like runs of seeds
in the leaf of the Judas tree.
A large tarp was placed on the ground
then all of us in our sleeping bags
and another tarp on top.

We woke to bird calls and wood smoke,
wallabies at the edge of the glade.
Too soon it would be time to move on
and sit on the wheel humps
inside the old red postie's van,
banged up together and complaining.

The Old House

Interiors are lost all the time. EDWARD HOLLIS

The dog ran in there.
It had been a mistake
to take his old trail.
He had picked up the scent
and bolted;
down the loved path,
through the painted green door
and the black and white tiled hall
to the room that opened out magisterially to the river.
Her grandmother's house
that her mother had inherited –
she only understood
the sweetness of that later
– but it was not to be hers or her sister's
for there stood the strange man
in his ripped low slung jeans,
the beginnings of red hair
she did not want to see
snaking up his muscled belly.
He turned and smiled
as if he could read it all
in an instant;
a lanky girl and her dog
who had hightailed it home
or what had once been home.
She was not ready for this ruin.

She was not ready for these feelings
that came at once together.
That she wanted to hit him.
That she wanted to kiss him.
The light drained out of the river then
and all the childish games and dances
she had devised in that room
dived away like nymphs.
You can stay a while you know, he'd said.
But she was out and away with the dog,
pelting down the now foreign shape
of the path on which she had learned to crawl.

From the Queensway

No space is big enough for you
my thrift-shop Boadicea
with your Russian fringe.
You stride through tunnels,
past the posters of Hedda Gabler
with her eyebrows solidly
graffitied in.
On the tube
your hennaed hand
keeps time
to God knows what tunes.
Get your own music –
the old joke between us.
Next to you
the soulful boy
inclines his head
to listen in.
You hide your hand
so he can't read
your ying/yang moon/stars
but he alights whistling
anyway the gift you've given him
unawares.

A Bourne

When I was a child I was always lying on the earth
as if some force pulled me there to know it.
And then it was with boys – two bodies drawn
by gravities they did not understand.
There was a moment in feeling entire,
the night-sky so close, it was my coat.
But when my own children came some brute separation happened.
I had to give this lying down to them. I was banished to stand
or squat, sometimes running my fingers over foreign ground
to find the spot that might pull me down again.
Death seemed lovely, the secret promise of a last embrace.
I wrapped and wrapped a small homunculus in my mind.

As it often happens, on an ordinary day
we drove out to Chudalup,
and climbed and climbed till thought left our limbs.
Our children were off, free,
crouching at rock-pools,
throwing their arms to the sky.
When all were quiet and out of sight I felt a patch
of rock, warm to its core.
There was a deep time through it – no – it was
particularities – tiny specs of mica, lichen weaving
its patterns and wholly indifferent to the way
it dug at my skin or how water tasted licked off its wounds.
A whole unschooled knowledge of place streamed in
and the liquid vision of boatmen,

was mine in constellations.
Just in this moment the way the planet turned
moved through the axis of my bones.
The white worm in my mind shrivelled and died.
I went to ground, pinned myself, palms down,
to this bourne, this fold in the earth,
held all our voices and footsteps in its spin.

This Only

She rode to the abandoned house,
and getting up good speed,
she flirted with butterflies,
forgot about her hair.
Here, she would roll up her sleeves
and make an Eden for them both;
only this time
they would get it right.
So, when she had fought
the damp and the dodgy wiring,
and started on the mural in his bedroom,
she remembered to paint out the apple tree.
She had decided, you see, on the ride,
that if there was to be fruit for the picking
it would do for their jam at breakfast and
this only.

3

I don't know why we need to live in bodies

KERRY HARDIE, 'Life Gone Away is Called Death'

The French Film

The evening we came home
from the French film
with Fanny Ardant saying
changez changez emphatically
I went to the bathroom mirror
and pinned up my hair.
It was the same mirror
in which we could see
parts of us making love
and we would sigh sometimes
and say *ah that's us*.
It was in the borrowed house
with the mournful cowbell
on the verandah
and the bedroom
in which we both felt
something terrible had happened.
But back then we were too young
to understand fully
what that might have been.

The Guardians

I could not bear the empyrean capped,
not after living so long under the ground.

You were away
when I found the lump.
You came back with a wooden duck
and a black toy dog.
In the thick of it
the duck would come to live
with the small plastic shepherd
and the stone our daughter found out in the river –
its shape sat safe in my hands.
The piggy bank was another gift.
My friend said put a coin in it a day
and smash it when you need to buy the dress
for your daughter's wedding.
But the dog – the dog was quite something.
Being stuffed, it said nothing.
In a dream it sat quietly by our own living dog
and she looked at me straight out of her old eyes and said
Go on – it's OK to pick it up.

Right Through Me

Little mortal,
afraid of all the sounds that
see into my body, afraid
of the techo's patient gaze
at the big screen where
Mr Muerto might be playing.
When they pin me to the plasma
the bony bit of me is tiny
with one perfect stone, is it,
or knot from some ancient accident?
Can you remember any trauma?
they ask, and I want to say
childhood falls from trees,
delirious, just because you could,
and being pulled roughly back
from dreaming on the Capri funicular.
But I just shrug
and feel the rightness
of withholding these lived jolts that
go right through me.

The Deer

This is the waiting room
at the place
where they shine you up.
The radiographer's face
is a smiling lesser sun
tracking between the two small moons
of her tattoos;
one between her breasts,
one beside her armpit.
Some get them clipped out
but for her they will always be ritual points,
the dye seeping in, Egyptian blue.
Why don't they make them brown like moles?
her oncologist tutted,
but she loved the blue.

In the same waiting room
she falls into a scene in a book,
deer moving in a glade
(low lights, the institutional carpet,
everyone's quiet moves)
and the words remembered
– they don't do that to their own –
are unrecoverable now,
or the whole around them.

What did they mean
at this particular meeting point?
What did she take them to mean
as she folded them under
the blue tattoos, sternum straight?

Yes, she was with the herd
in the dapple
and had been hurt
but no one was to blame.
Keep moving with them all, she thought.
Trust the dollar-shop stickers
– the lady birds and love hearts –
on the giant roving lights;
and the nurses' soft talk
as she sat up.
When it was all over
she never went back
to find the book
but left those words
– *they don't do that to their own* –
for others to work out.

Driving to the First

The time of my illness is lost.
It has died its own death.
I can't remember what
the each of us
must have been thinking
when we lay side by side
all those nights through it.
Though one thing sticks –
a conversation at the lights we had
when driving to the first chemotherapy
(I say this word in full
not to get too friendly with it).
We were driving to the first
and the day felt as big as
a trip by sea, uncertain, expansive.
You turned and told me
of a strange contentment
that had just seized you.
Despite everything
it seemed to fit.
And when you asked how I felt back
I said like the goat stuck in the mud
in the art book we'd left spread out on our bed
and also that I suddenly wanted…
I suddenly wanted so much
I could not name or place.

Eve

Eve is my doctor.
She tells me every year
that I am doing OK.
I walk back to the car
by the artificial lake.
I don't park underground.
The illness itself
was enough of a burial.
I look at the birdlife,
the trees, shabby
in the time of my treatment,
that have recovered now.
I say the name Eve
to the water, the sky, the birds,
the footpath and the parking meter;
and each time it is as if
I am the first speaking woman
on earth.

Here

there is something comforting about sitting here with my hand
on Robert's breast
he says, here, steady yourself against me here, he says, after
a pause, he is thinking how best
to fit me, he says it must have been bad but you're here,
you're with us
the surroundings burst with surgical fittings
it all looks very Weimar, very *neue Sach*
I expect fishnets, a crossed-leg, a trail of cigar smoke somewhere
but there is only Robert and me and all the boxes
and Robert saying again, here, steady yourself against me here.

The Hammock

Your son found it
standing to your waist's height
in the bathroom
because it recalled
an illustration from *Gray's* –
That's not right…
Afterwards you lay
in the hammock in the sun,
one hand cupping
a prosthesis made of birdseed.
When you stood
it sat just so.
The hammock was always in your head
and at first, at night,
you were aware of its empty curve
as one might be of a philosophical conundrum.
There in the dark it was an uncertain smile,
the tree behind its nose, the stars, eyes;
the space aligned, you came to think,
with what had been removed.
But then when you climbed
in it again by daylight
you inhabited it fully.

Saint Catherine's, Abbotsbury

For Aaron

I made a covert pilgrimage
up the worn path
through the strip lynchets
and indifferent sheep
until the ruin of Saint Catherine's
small buttressed magnitude
was gained;
a place that was, you said much later,
held together by bits of paper,
feathers, shells and prayers.
Perfect acoustics, you marvelled,
as I searched for something silent
I could hear:
the thin note
I posted in a crevice
months ago,
and found the very same
in another voice.
Anchored beneath candle butts, weathered stones,
and here it was the same plaint
the same *I've been away, not myself,*
unwell, or my child, my love or
I must bear it all.
How could I tell you
what it felt like to be back and well.
The midden crunched beneath our feet.

We left its hush
for those great outer walls
and found a sheltered corner
where mustard-coloured lichen clung.
You said that this was perhaps one of my colours
and I took the whole place in,
sucked calm into my lungs,
pocketed a chalky stone.

A Renovation (Girl's Work)

I've always had a fascination with the needle…The magic power of the needle. The needle is used to repair the damage. LOUISE BOURGEOIS

I have decided
that I will start mending
and that only my hands
will suffice.
I will, I know, get furious
with my limitations
but then there is something so
beautiful about the flawed work
human hands can do.
It will hold;
for think of a time
when only this labour
covered the body.
Can you imagine the tedium,
punctuated by the bright flairs
of the company of others,
the sheer graft of it, those calloused thumbs.
Also, an early memory of my mother's:
pointless work snatched from small hands
hot with a summer's day,
the teacher's voice admonishing
that this girl's work,
(*look at it!*)
is the worst
in the whole class.

Your Paintings

i.m. Noel Dougan

More and more I live with your paintings
or more precisely the moment
you first saw them and chose them:
the red bird sitting in
the round of its glade;
the woman who has become
a train trip and a forest
as if her memory were a strip of film
containing both.

The man who helped you choose the paintings
had a name that sounded
like a small animal.
He was the same man
who persuaded you
that instant coffee
tasted better with the milk
stirred in first.

Every few weeks
I buy the cheapest tinned coffee,
come home, and stir it with that spoon of his.
With each motion
I sense your careful steps around the gallery.
You halt here, you halt there,
waiting for the lady with the coloured dots

on the ends of her fingers
to close the deal
on the red bird
and the woman who is becoming
both a trip by train
and a forest.

Bump & Grind

For Neil and Beth

For weeks after the dance concert
our daughter's costume drifts above us
in the dining room;
an explosion in pink rosebuds and tulle,
weightless as Nijinsky's leap.

When we walk beneath it
we hold our breath
yet it is not ethereality I feel from it
but sweat and effort,
the earthiness and earthed-ness of dancing,
the on and off love affair
we've had with your dance school:
tacky costumes and make-up,
the relentless bump and grind
foisted on the younger girls.
Still the dance mistress was kind
and when you were tired she'd say
to sit on the edge and watch
(*you can learn a lot like that, girls*).
It was always the better performance,
seeing all of you draped one against the other.

Before the lessons end
you ask me to pack away the dress.
Much later you'll slash the tutu,

wear it over jeans,
and I will harvest the rose buds
of which the sewing on
gave me so many small wounds,
and they'll get dusty in a red cup
on my desk
the year that you start bleeding
and I stop.

After You Shout

After you shout at the child
we drive past pine branches
stacked on the side of the road
and I want to make a home
of these materials
in which she can live.
You will be faraway
or incommoded as in tales.
Between here and there
is a modest upstairs flat lit low.
It's not clear that this is my new life,
not clear that I can build the pine shelter
and leave it for her – or that
this is what the shelter becomes in the day.
The music playing is diegetic
but it's a sound
that does not suit us all.

Turtle Love

For Tim

After a hopeless phone-call
you soak in the bath
consoling yourself with
the poem of the day.
I can imagine the tub
is too short for your legs
and the deft way you manage
not to get the newspaper wet.
Between us, all those wires,
all that water, not much said.
So when you post me Dyer's old lines
I think of his turtles as emissaries,
hauling their awkwardness
through sea miles,
an entirely silent progress,
steadfast by sonic maps.
It's only later that I learn
to love your unspent rhyme.
His turtles are not turtles.
They are doves.

Dearest

The word dearest
opens the door
to another century
where a man might stoop
to adjust a woman's errant shawl.
And dearest in that time
begins letters, too,
that travelled distances in carriages
over fields in all weathers
to be received in agitation
or with calm
once their waxy seals were broken.
And even dearest blinking on the screen
sent snaking by hidden phone lines
can still contain this whole century,
the trailing shawl, the man and
the woman poised for this moment
of rearrangement and then,
forgetting us, they turn away.

A Picture from Julia

Now I need your Spring
as I never did when it was simply mine.
You've drawn me a very wintry picture.
My hair is charcoal, the heavens rain down
three cold things all at once
but that's OK.
I endure in the shelter your pencil has granted me,
looking back from the hollow of a ruin tree
to your luxuriant tendrils, your off-the-shoulder number,
your *quattrocento* lawn.
If anyone should take this green off me
I will summon the harpies,
set all of Campania alight;
and not rest
until the white button daisies return
and your feet make
a path through the thaw.

This project has been assisted by the Commonwealth Government through the Australia Council, its arts funding and advisory body.